Dear Parent:

Do you want to spark your child's creativity? Do you want your child to become a confident writer? Road to Writing can help.

Road to Writing is a unique creative writing program that gives even the youngest writers a chance to express themselves. Featuring five distinct levels, or Miles, the Road to Writing program accompanies children from their first attempts at writing to comfortably writing on their own.

A Creative Start
For children who "write" stories by drawing pictures
• easy picture prompts • familiar subjects • places to draw

Creative Writing With Help
For children who write easy words with help
• detailed picture prompts • places to draw and label

Creative Writing On Your Own
For children who write simple sentences on their own
• basic story starters • popular topics • places to write

First Journals
For children who are comfortable writing short paragraphs
• more complex story starters • space for free writing

Journals
For children who want to try different kinds of writing
• cues for poems, jokes, stories • brainstorming pages

There's no need to hurry through the Miles. Road to Writing is designed without age or grade levels. Children can progress at their own speed, developing confidence and pride in their writing ability along the way.

Road to Writing—"write" from the start!

Road to Writing

books

Mile 1

Cool School
Super Me!

Mile 2

Boo!
Road Trip

Mile 3

Monkey Business
Sports Shorts

Tips for Using this Book

- Let your child read each page and write a response—right in the book!
- Don't worry about spelling or penmanship. Just let your child enjoy the experience of capturing ideas on paper.
- Remind your child to write at his or her own pace. There's no rush!
- Encourage your child with plenty of praise.

Pencils, pens, and crayons are all suitable for use in this book. Markers are not recommended.

A GOLDEN BOOK • New York
Golden Books Publishing Company, Inc. New York, New York 10106

ISBN: 0-307-45406-1 R MCMXCIX

SPORTS SHORTS

by Sarah Albee and

____

(your name)

illustrated by
Mike Lester and

____

(your name)

Not long ago. . .

(Circle the ones you want in your story.)

I was playing

soccer

softball

basketball

in a

swamp

stadium

schoolyard

against a team of

giants.

fierce pirates.

Olympic athletes.

Write what happened next.

All of a sudden, ____________________

____

____

____

Then, ____________________

____

____

____

Finally, ____________________

____

____

____

Make up an ad for a prune-flavored sports drink.

What is it called?

What is special about it?

Write a sentence that will make people want to buy the drink.

Draw your ad here.

You're going one-on-one with a professional basketball player!

Write down your game plan.

Step 1: ______________________________

____

Step 2: ______________________________

____

Step 3: ______________________________

____

Step 4: ______________________________

____

Draw yourself following one of the steps.

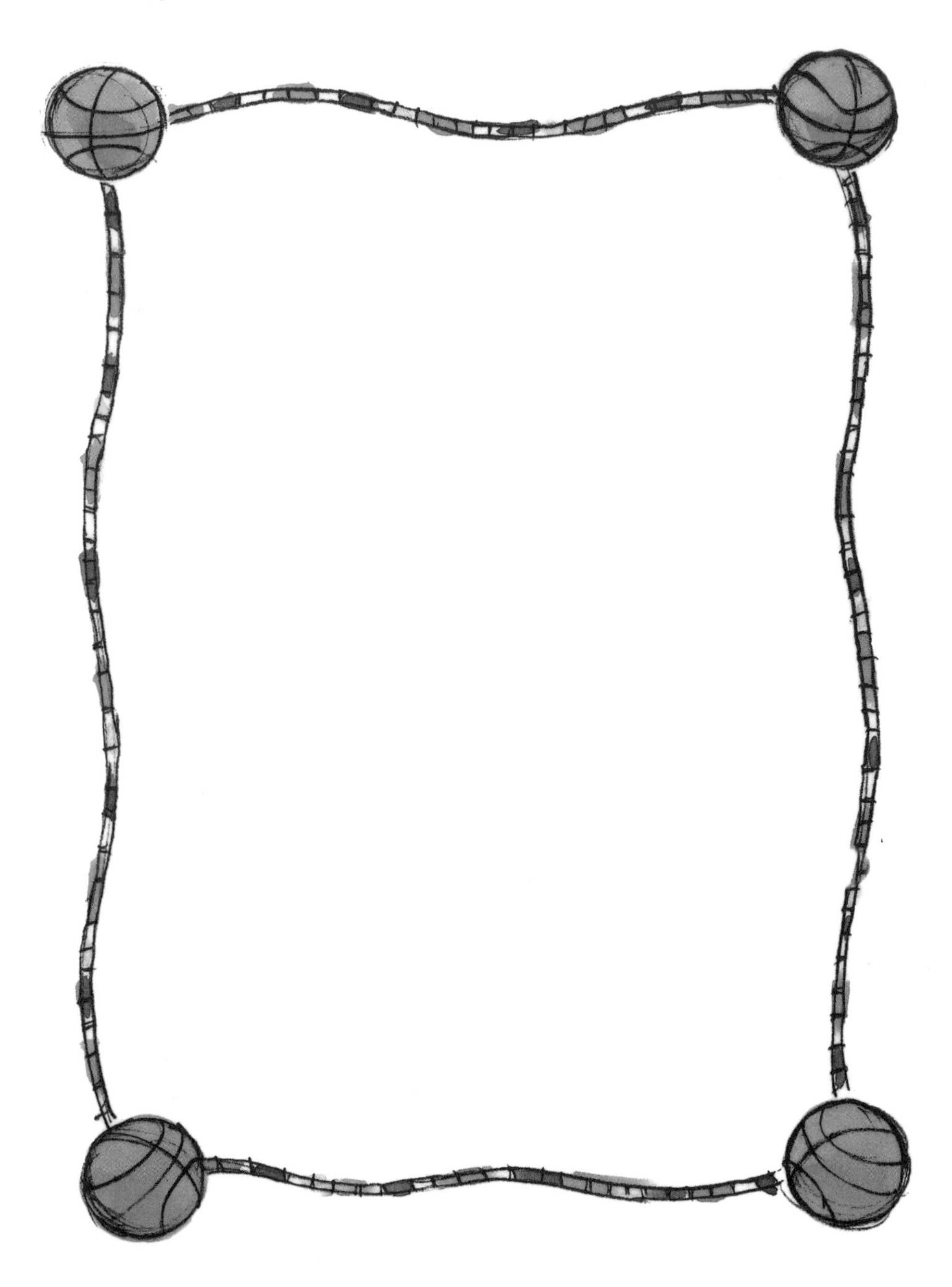

Sports I'm good at:

Sports I'd like to get better at:

Fill in the caption.
Then finish the cartoon.
"The bad news is
________________.
The good news is
________________."

You're a reporter for
SPORTS BLOOPERS.
Finish the article about this blooper.

★Sports Bloopers★

____

(Title of your article)

Today at the ice rink, ______________________________

____

____

____

After she was pulled out of the water, the skater said,

"______________________________

______________________________!"

Invent a new sport.

What kind of equipment do you need?

What are the rules?

How do you decide who wins?

Draw a picture of yourself playing this new sport.

What sport do you play each season?

Describe what you like about each sport.

FALL SPORT:

____

I like it because ______________________

____

____

WINTER SPORT:

____

I like it because ______________________

____

____

SPRING SPORT:

____

I like it because ______________________________

____

____

SUMMER SPORT:

____

I like it because ______________________________

____

____

It's the ninth inning.
You're up at bat.
Your team needs just one run
to win the championship!
The pitcher throws the ball.

Write the rest of the story.

You swing and ______________________________

____

____

____

____

SPRING SPORT:

____

I like it because______________________

____

____

SUMMER SPORT:

____

I like it because______________________

____

____

It's the ninth inning.
You're up at bat.
Your team needs just one run
to win the championship!
The pitcher throws the ball.

Write the rest of the story.

You swing and ____________________________

____

____

____

____

Draw a picture to illustrate your story.

Make up an ad for a new kind of sneakers.

What are they called?

What is special about them?

Write a sentence that will make people want to buy the sneakers.

Draw your ad here.

The big race just ended!
Let's hear from the winner.

Tortoise: "________________________________

____

____

____."

And now a question for the loser.

Hare: "______________________________

____

____

______________________________."

Uncle Henry just sent you:
(Circle one.)

his favorite
golf club

a bike helmet with
duckies on it

a picture of him
riding his unicycle

Write a thank-you note.

Write at least three nice things about the gift.

(date)

Dear Uncle Henry,

Love,

MY FANTASY STADIUM

If you could build a sports stadium in your backyard, what would it be like? Describe it.

Draw a picture of your fantasy stadium.

Fill in the caption.
Then finish the cartoon.

"I don't like to lift weights.

I like to lift ______________________________!"

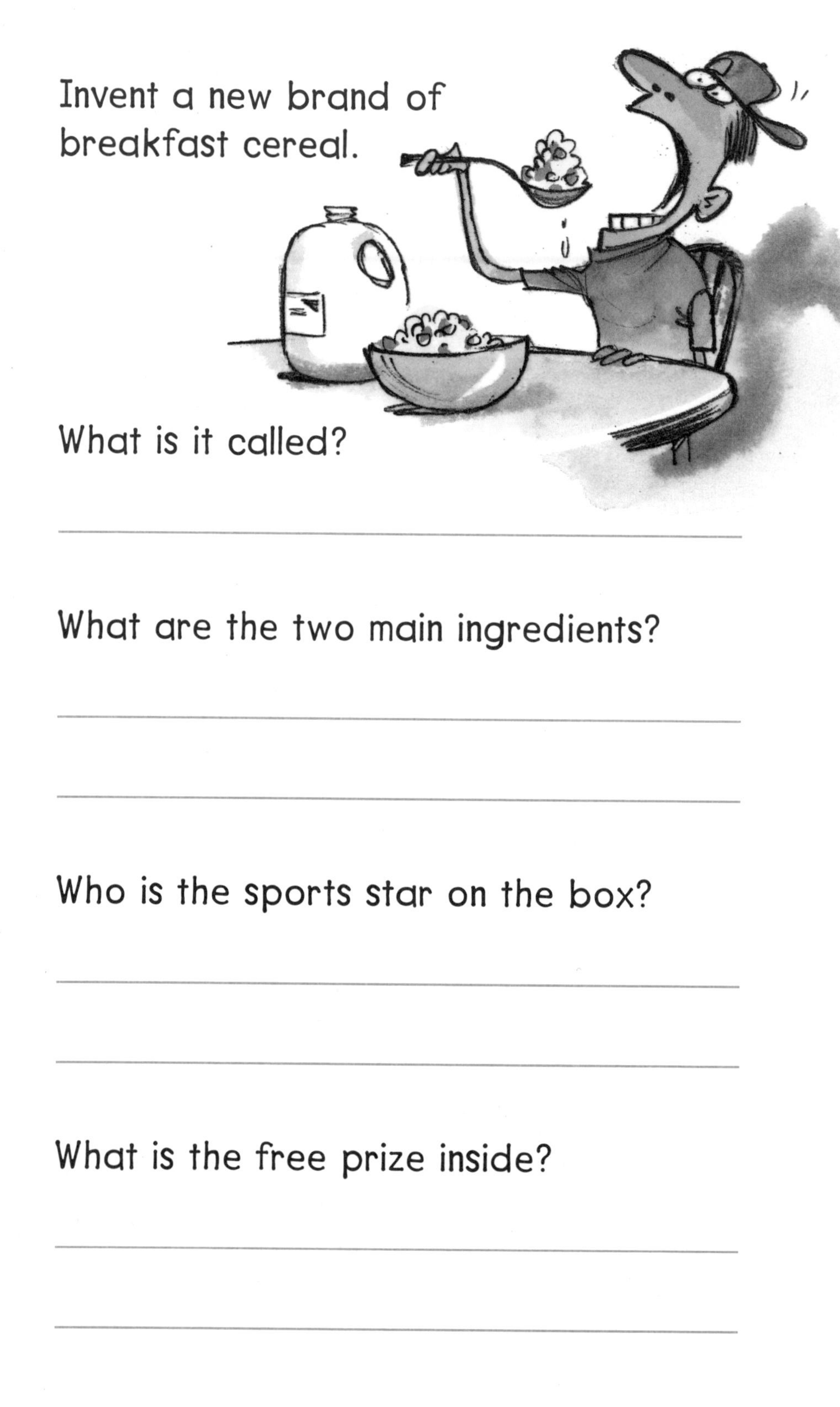

Invent a new brand of breakfast cereal.

What is it called?

____

What are the two main ingredients?

____

____

Who is the sports star on the box?

____

____

What is the free prize inside?

____

____

Design the box.

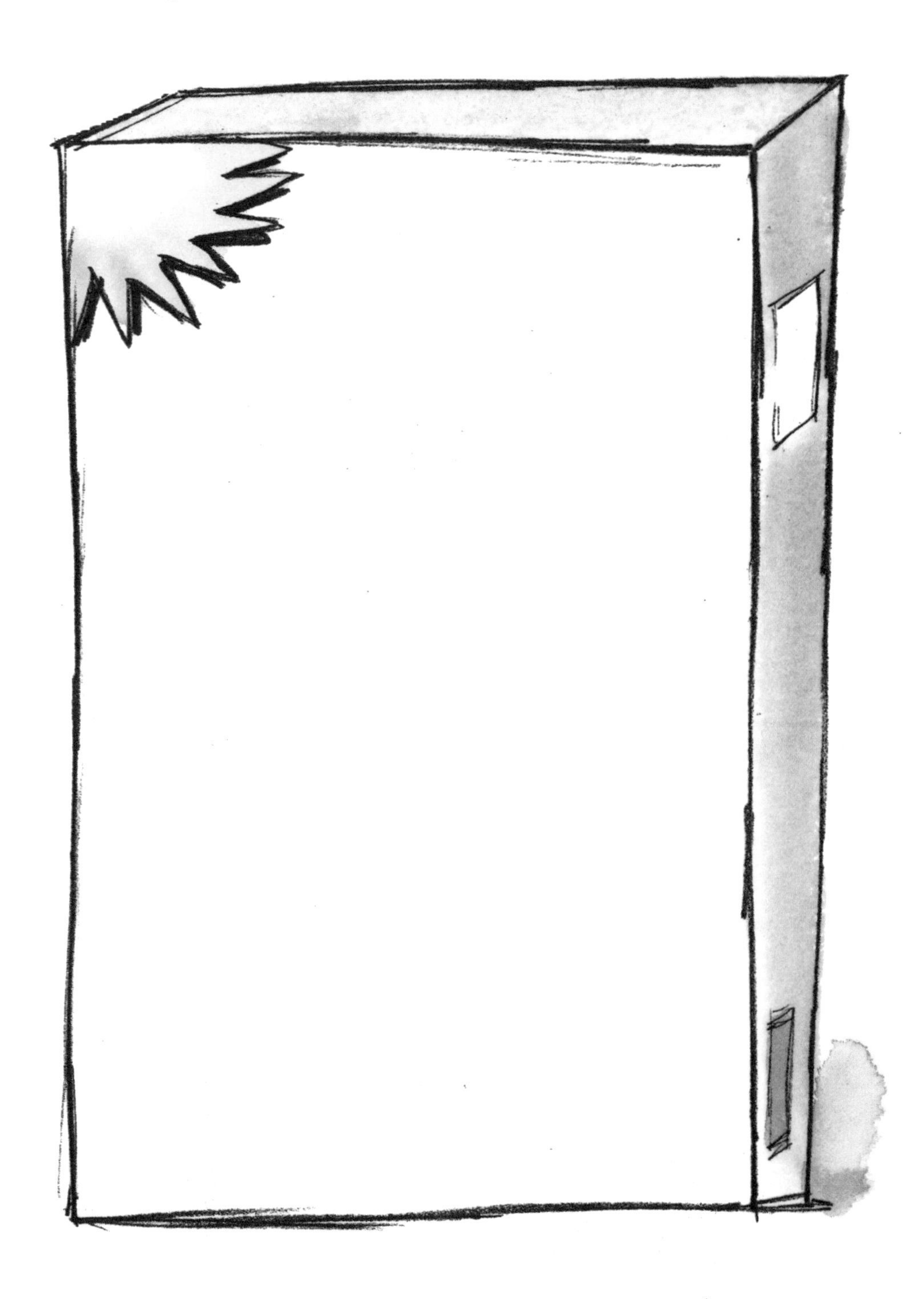

If you became a millionaire sports star, what's the first thing you would buy?

Draw it.

What does it do?

Why did you want it?

Who else will use it?

Fill in the caption.

"I have a better idea, fellas.

Let's ______________________________!"

Draw what happens next.

Write the caption.

"

____

____!"

You're the announcer for the

Outerspace Olympics!

Finish describing this event.

"And they're off!

Iggle Bish from Mars is in the lead.

But wait! Here comes ____________________

____

____

____

And the winner is:

____!"

Write a letter to your favorite sports star.

____
(date)

Dear __________________________,

____

____

____

____

____

Sincerely,

____

Draw a picture of you meeting your favorite sports star.

Fill in the caption.
Then finish the cartoon.
"Look! It's a
_______________!"
TOP

Start your own Iron-Kid Triathalon.

First event: ______________________________

____

Second event: ______________________________

____

Third event: ______________________________

____

Draw one of the events.

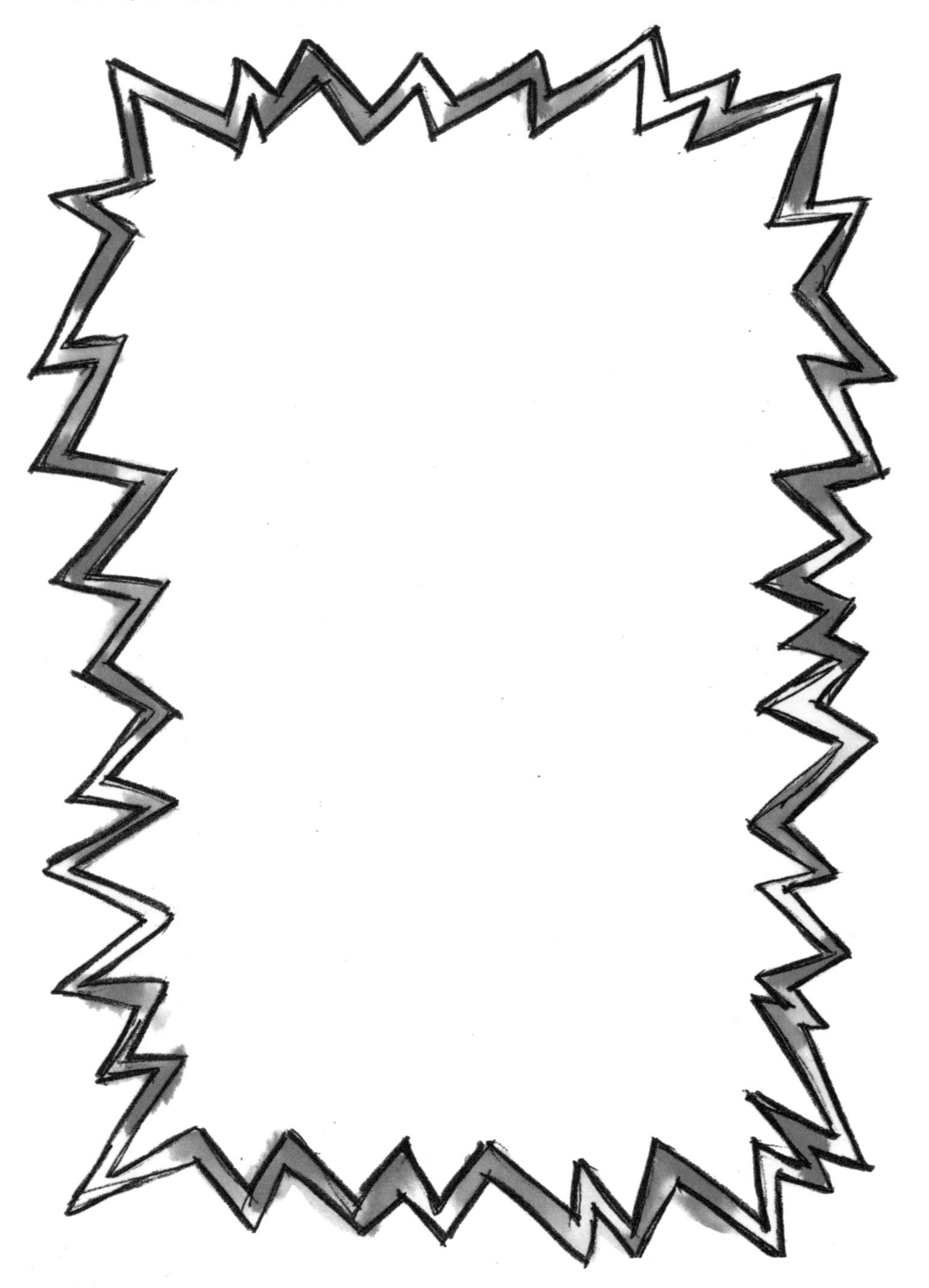

Draw yourself receiving an Olympic gold medal.

What event did you win?